Goose berry Patch ™

the Country Friends Collection ™

At Home

Mary
Kate Elizabeth

Holly

Holly

···hand·painted mailboxes for everybody in the neighborhood.

···subscribes to 28 different decorating magazines and can't bear to throw any of them away.

···has painted her front door a dozen times this year, everytime a different color!

♥ MARY ELIZABETH'S ♥
LITTLE TOUCHES THAT

PUT OUT tHE WELCOME MAT!

♥ bird houses

♥ an old rocker on the porch

♥ Welcome mats or rag rugs by the door

♥ wooden benches

♥ hand-painted front door or wooden screen door

HOME ♥ SWEET ♥ HOME

♥ shutters on the windows

♥ windchimes singing in the breeze

♥ a wreath or door swag

♥ a porch swing piled up with pillows

♥ a lazy old dog sleeping on the porch

♥ Potted plants & topiaries

"NOT MANY SOUNDS IN LIFE ... EXCEED IN INTEREST A KNOCK AT THE DOOR. —CHARLES LAMB, 1775-1834

2

Wonderful & Welcoming Entrances

Mary Elizabeth has been dreaming of an entrancing entryway... the hardest part is choosing!

CHECKERBOARD TRIM WITH A LIGHT WASH OF STAIN OVER IT FOR AN ANTIQUED LOOK... *a definite possibility.*

412

A PRETTY STENCILED WREATH RIGHT ON THE DOOR... ACCENT STENCILED DESIGNS ON EACH CORNER... *a good idea!*

ENTER WITH A HAPPY HEART

HAND-LETTER A FAVORITE SLOGAN ON THE DOOR TRIM... *unique!*

Welcome

A RED DOOR WITH NAVY SHUTTERS & AMERICANA DECORATIONS... *neat!*

Hello!

A QUICK COAT OF GLOSSY GREEN ON THE DOOR ~ A BASKET OF BLOOMS & IVY HAND-PAINTED ON THE TRIM.... *yes!*

Hmmm....

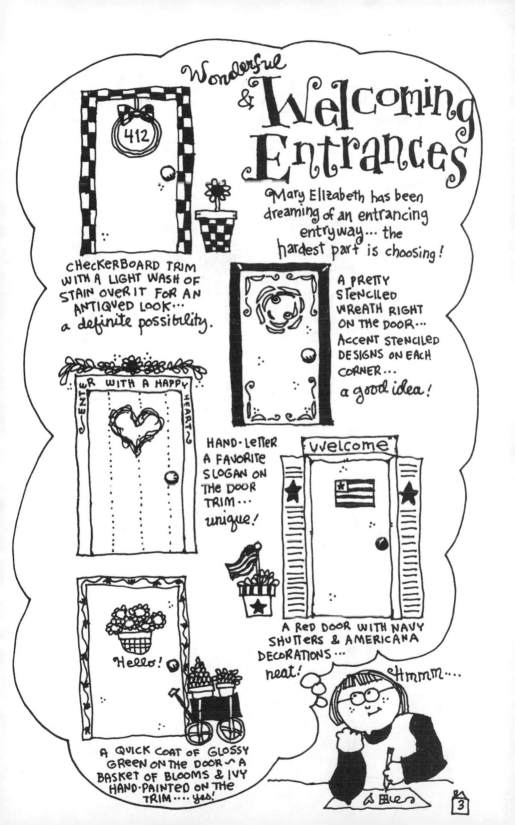

3

Message Box

...handy when nobody's home!

YOU'LL NEED:
- WOODEN BOX OR BASKET WITH LID
- SUPPLIES TO DECORATE BOX OR BASKET SUCH AS PAINT, RIBBONS, DECOUPAGE ITEMS
- NOTEBOOK
- PEN

Leave a message

Hello! Call me later. –Spot

#1. DECORATE THE BOX OR BASKET AS YOU WISH TO COORDINATE WITH YOUR HOUSE.

#2. PLACE THE FOLLOWING MESSAGE ON THE LID OR PRINT ON A WOODEN CUT-OUT YOU CAN HANG ON THE BASKET:

> Leave a message if you like, In the morning, noon or night!

#3. HANG OR PLACE MESSAGE BOX OR BASKET NEXT TO THE FRONT DOOR WITH A NOTEBOOK & PEN INSIDE.

ROVER

Wonderful Window·Boxes

a simple window·box full of whimsy can change the whole look of your home! Just add a new collection of goodies with each season's arrival. Some ideas to get you started, courtesy of Holly:

winter — EVERGREEN BOUGHS, LONG TWIGS & FROSTY SNOWMEN IN A WINDOW BOX SETTING WILL SEE YOU THROUGH WINTER'S CHILL...

Spring — ...'TIL YOU'RE READY FOR SPRING. RE·FILL YOUR BOX WITH A BED OF SPHAGNUM MOSS. ADD FORSYTHIA BRANCHES AND EASTER EGGS — PERHAPS A BUNNY TO PEEK OVER, TOO!

summer — WARM WEATHER CALLS FOR REAL FLOWERS & HERBS. A COLLECTION OF TINY BIRDHOUSES WILL LOOK GREAT!

autumn — A HARVEST OF PUMPKINS, GOURDS & APPLES IN A STRAW BED WELCOMES FALL.

A small house well~filled is better than an empty palace.
— THOMAS HALIBURTON

Painted Mailboxes

Enhance the beauty of a plain old box!

YOU WILL NEED:

- MAILBOX ~ PLAIN OR PAINTED
- OUTDOOR ENAMEL PAINTS
- PAINT BRUSHES (3" FOAM, STENCIL & SMALL ROUND)
- STENCILS
- MASKING TAPE

HOW TO:

IF YOU CHOOSE A PLAIN MAILBOX, PAINT IN DESIRED COLOR USING 3" FOAM BRUSH. LET DRY.

PLACE STENCIL ON MAILBOX ~ SECURE WITH MASKING TAPE. LOAD STENCIL BRUSH WITH PAINT ~ BLOT EXCESS ON PAPER TOWEL BEFORE STENCILING. WITH A LIGHT DABBING MOTION, APPLY PAINT FROM OUTSIDE EDGES OF THE STENCIL DESIGN, WORKING IN TOWARD CENTER.

REMEMBER, TOO, THAT WHEN USING MORE THAN 1 COLOR IN A DESIGN, IT'S IMPORTANT TO LET EACH COLOR DRY BEFORE ADDING ANOTHER.

GENTLY REMOVE STENCIL FROM MAILBOX. EMBELLISH DESIGN WITH HAND-PAINTED DETAILS IF DESIRED.

FOLKART, STAMPING OR FAUX FINISHES MAY ALSO BE USED ON YOUR MAILBOX. BE CREATIVE ~ HAVE FUN!

make a Delightful Designer SISAL RUG

YOU WILL NEED:

SISAL RUG
RULER OR CARPENTER'S SQUARE
MASKING TAPE
PAINT, ACRYLIC OR ENAMEL
BRUSHES
SPONGES
STAMPS
FABRIC ~ OPTIONAL
MATCHING THREAD ~ OPTIONAL
CURVED UPHOLSTERY NEEDLE ~
            OPTIONAL

1. Make a rough sketch of your design on a piece of paper.

2. Mark off area to be painted using a ruler & masking tape.

3. Apply design to rug using paint, stencils, stamps or sponging.

Cut fabric into 6-to-8-inch wide strips, depending on size of the rug.

4. Let paint dry overnight before removing masking tape.

5. You can add a fabric border at this point, if you like ~ choose a fabric to coordinate with other items in the room.

6. With an iron, press a 1-inch hem along each long side of the strip. Next, fold strip in half with wrong sides together. Press.

7. Place folded strip of fabric over the rug edges and sew into place.

7

Collec

OH, THE THRILL OF THE HUNT! LOOKING FOR THAT CERTAIN SOMETHING AT FLEA MARKETS & ANTIQUE SHOWS IS FUN. HERE ARE A FEW IDEAS TO GET YOU GOING.

QUILTS

POTTERY

TEA POTS

COOKIE JARS

POSTCARDS

BIRDHOUSES

SPOONS

SALT & PEPPER SHAKERS

DOLLS

ANTIQUE TOYS

GARAGE SALE TODAY

NAUTICAL ITEMS

VASES

t·i·o·n·s

FROM THE COUNTRY FRIENDS™. JUST REMEMBER...
LOOK FOR THINGS THAT TICKLE YOUR FANCY, MAKE YOU
SMILE, AND WILL FIT IN YOUR HOUSE!

VINTAGE JEWELRY

OLD BEARS

OLD GARDEN THINGS

AMERICANA

ANIMAL FIGURINES

OLD KITCHEN ITEMS

NEEDLEPOINT

DOLLHOUSES

BABY PLATES & CUPS

ALPHABET BLOCKS

PEWTER & COPPER

LACE & LINENS

SHOWGLOBES

COUNTRY FRIENDS HINT: DON'T COLLECT THE SAME THING AS YOUR FRIENDS COLLECT.

TABLESCAPES
A GREAT WAY TO DISPLAY COLLECTIONS

TIE TOGETHER YOUR DISPLAYS BY STICKING TO A THEME, WHETHER IT BE ON A TABLETOP OR IN A CUPBOARD!

Some Country Friends™ Favorites:

garden goodies

SMALL WATERING CAN
POTTED FLOWERS
NOSEGAYS IN A PRETTY BOWL
SMALL GARDEN STATUES
GARDEN URNS & POTS
FLORAL TABLECLOTH
OLD RAKE TO PROP UP AS BACKDROP
BASKET OR BOWL OF NATURE
    ITEMS ~ EGGS, PINECONES &
    UNUSUAL LEAVES, FOR
    EXAMPLE
POTPOURRI

Book Nook

OLD BOOKS TIED UP WITH
    A RIBBON
MINIATURE PICTURE FRAMES
OLD-FASHIONED MAGNIFYING
    GLASS
SMALL EASEL WITH A
    LITTLE PAINTING
GLASS PAPERWEIGHTS
VARIOUS INTERESTING
    SMALL BOXES
OLD LAMP OR LANTERN

Kitchen Collection

CROCK OF CINNAMON STICKS
BOWL OF FRUIT
GLASS JARS OF WHOLE SPICES
ANTIQUE KITCHEN UTENSILS
ROLLING PINS
STONEWARE CROCKERY
HOMESPUN TOWELS
OLD COOKIE CUTTERS &
    ANTIQUE COOKBOOKS

Seaside Summer

WHITE-WASHED TABLE
SHELLS & STARFISH
FISHNETTING
PITCHERS IN BLUE,
  YELLOW OR WHITE
ANTIQUE SANDPAILS &
  SHOVELS
BIG CLEAR FISHBOWL
  TO FILL WITH SAND
   & SHELLS
WHITE WICKER
  BASKETS
INTERESTING DRIFTWOOD
SAILBOATS
VACATION PHOTOS

♥I know not why, but home is dearest. ～CICERO 106-43 B.C.

11

Be Our Guest!

For the Bath:

a basket of goodies like bubble bath, soap, shampoos & lotions

GEL

SOAP

terry cloth robes

a hair dryer

packaged toothbrushes & toothpaste

SMILE BRITE

a stack of extra towels & washcloths

a peg rack to hang clothes & towels on

pamper your guests with these simple touches from Holly & her country friends™

a bath pillow

12

For the Bedroom:

a reading lamp

copies of favorite books, magazines & papers

Goose Berry Patch
Jane Eyre
Love Story

a water pitcher & cups

a clock

a bowl of fresh fruit

fresh flowers

scented candles & matches

padded hangers in the closet

radio, tape or CD player with favorite music

paper, pen & stationery items
Hello!

a bed tray

extra pillows & blankets

mending kit

a flower box at the window

herbal sleep pillow

iron & ironing board in closet

a tea pot or electric kettle & a basket of teabags & instant coffees & cocoas

a comfortable chair for reading

THIS IS THE LIFE...
I'M never Leaving!

STenciled SHeet Set

...make your own designer sheets!

the most beautiful place on Earth, our childhood home. - Peggy Jones

YOU WILL NEED:

* SOLID COLOR SHEET SET WITH MATCHING PILLOWCASES
* FABRIC PAINTS OR ACRYLICS MIXED WITH TEXTILE MEDIUM
* FABRIC PAINT PENS
* RIBBON OR LACE TRIM ~ OPTIONAL

1. Select a border design stencil to make this project super-simple.

2. Stencil design on finished edge of flat sheet & pillow cases. Let dry.

3. With fabric marker, write a special message like "Sweet Dreams."

4. Add ribbon or lace trim if desired.

* If you're feeling especially creative, use rubber stamps or stencils to continue the designwork all over the sheet!

sweet · dreams · sweetie

☆ easy
Duvet ☆
☆ Cover

YOU WILL NEED:

* 2 FLAT SHEETS, CONTRASTING FABRICS
* PAPER-BACKED FUSIBLE WEB TAPE
* BUTTONS, SNAPS OR HOOK-AND-LOOP TAPE

1. Wash sheets to remove sizing.

2. Place right sides of sheets together. Lay duvet on top of sheets ~ the top of the duvet should come within about an inch of the wide hem edge of sheets. Fuse sides & bottom seams together with fusible web tape following instructions on package.

3. Turn cover right-side out. Slip over duvet. Close open end with buttons, snaps or hook-and-loop tape.
~ Cover up!

sweet dre...

Mary Elizabeth's
GOOD IDEAS ☆

Make a flannel duvet cover for the chilly months out of cozy flannel sheets!

Kids love the idea of personalized sheets. Decorate a set according to our directions (opposite page) with a stars-and-moon design and add your child's name on the edging. Make a matching duvet cover with the same starry night motif...and stencil stars on your kid's walls with glow-in-the-dark paint! They'll look forward to bed-time in their star-lit retreat. ☆ ☾ ☆

For a neat tailored look, buy two fitted sheets ~ one for the mattress and one to cover the box springs on your bed.

☆

Stenciled sheets make great gifts for newlyweds or for a house-warming gift.

Sleep tight! ☆

They can lift your spirits... make you rest easier... Inspire you to new creative heights ~ **Colors!**

Choose carefully as you decide on color schemes for your home, as your decisions may affect your entire well-being! For instance:

◆ **Red, Orange & Yellow** rev us up, stimulate creativity & lift our spirits.

◆ **Blue, Purple & Pink** help to relax us & reduce stress.

◆ **Green,** has a warming effect, while **Blue** makes us feel cooler.

◆ **White** & light colors make us feel a sense of spaciousness ~ **Dark** colors will lend a feeling of coziness.

COLOR SCHEMING?

SOME HELPFUL GUIDELINES:

1. ask yourself: How much do I like this color? How soon will I get tired of looking at it?

☐ (A) I LOVE IT MORE THAN LIFE ITSELF.

☐ (B) THAT CHARTREUSE BATHROOM TILE SEEMED LIKE A GOOD IDEA AT THE TIME.

☐ (C) JUST POKE MY EYES OUT NOW AND PUT ME OUT OF MY MISERY.

★ **T**o BUILD A HOUSE IS ONE THING, BUT TO MAKE IT A **HOME** IS QUITE ANOTHER...

~ Louis L'Amour

AMERICAN WRITER

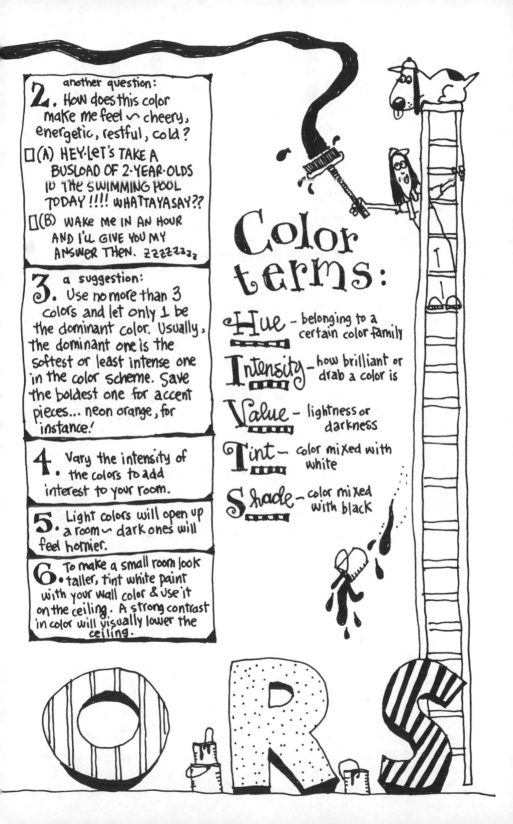

2. another question:
How does this color make me feel ∿ cheery, energetic, restful, cold?

☐ (A) HEY·LET's TAKE A BUSLOAD OF 2-YEAR-OLDS TO THE SWIMMING POOL TODAY!!!! WHATTAYASAY??

☐ (B) WAKE ME IN AN HOUR AND I'LL GIVE YOU MY ANSWER THEN. ZZZZZZzz

3. a suggestion:
Use no more than 3 colors and let only 1 be the dominant color. Usually, the dominant one is the softest or least intense one in the color scheme. Save the boldest one for accent pieces... neon orange, for instance!

4. Vary the intensity of the colors to add interest to your room.

5. Light colors will open up a room ∿ dark ones will feel homier.

6. To make a small room look taller, tint white paint with your wall color & use it on the ceiling. A strong contrast in color will visually lower the ceiling.

Color terms:

Hue – belonging to a certain color family

Intensity – how brilliant or drab a color is

Value – lightness or darkness

Tint – color mixed with white

Shade – color mixed with black

OFF THE

1. TRY THIS METHOD IF PAINTING & WALLPAPERING ARE NOT YOUR BAG ∽ VERY EASY TO DO IN A DAY! YOU WILL NEED:

* DECORATIVE SHEETS OR PIECES OF FABRIC
* STAPLE GUN
* DECORATIVE MOLDING
* PUSH PINS

USE STAPLE GUN TO ATTACH SHEETS OR FABRIC TO THE WALL. WHEN STAPLING, ADD SMALL FOLDS AT TOP SO SHEETS OR FABRIC HAVE A SOFT GATHERED LOOK INSTEAD OF FLAT & STIFF AGAINST THE WALL. AFTER STAPLING THE TOP, FINISH THE BOTTOM THE SAME WAY. ADD DECORATIVE MOLDING AT TOP & BOTTOM TO COVER STAPLES.

2. THE AMAZING KITCHEN SPONGE METHOD!

YOU NEED:
* SPONGES ∽ KITCHEN OR BOAT & DECK
* ACRYLIC PAINTS
* PLASTIC PLATE * PAPER TOWELS

CUT SPONGES INTO DESIRED SHAPES ∽ EASY ONES LIKE GEOMETRICS, STARS & HEARTS WORK BEST. DIP INTO WATER ∽ SQUEEZE OUT EXCESS ONTO PLATE. IT SHOULD BE DAMP, NOT SOAKING WET ∽ COVER SPONGE SURFACE WITH PAINT. BLOT EXCESS ON TOWEL, THEN STAMP WALL WITH SPONGE. RELOAD WITH PAINT AS NECESSARY. (TRY TO KEEP AMOUNT OF PAINT EVEN ON EACH SPONGED DESIGN.) LET DRY. PAINT OVER YOUR MASTERPIECE WITH NON-YELLOWING POLYURETHANE TO MAKE WALL WASHABLE. (THIS WORKS GREAT ON FURNITURE, TOO!)

WALL

3. GRAB YOUR TRUSTY DRYWALL KNIFE AND GET READY TO **TEXTURE!**

* DRYWALL JOINT COMPOUND
* TROWEL
* DRYWALL KNIFE
* TEXTURE TOOLS LIKE CRUMBLED PLASTIC BAGS, BROOMS, BRUSHES, OTHER UNIQUE THINGS YOU MIGHT FIND AROUND THE HOUSE

START WITH A CLEAN WALL, FREE OF DIRT & GREASE. IT'S A GOOD IDEA TO REPAIR ANY HOLES OR CRACKS BEFORE YOU START.

WITH A TROWEL, APPLY A 1/4" THICK LAYER OF DRYWALL JOINT COMPOUND. WORK IN SMALL AREAS AT A TIME.

ONCE THE WALL IS COVERED WITH COMPOUND, DRAG A DRYWALL KNIFE DOWN THE WALL TO SMOOTH IT OUT & PREPARE IT FOR TEXTURING. PRETEND YOU'RE ICING A CAKE. NOW YOU'RE READY TO ADD THE TEXTURING! CHOOSE YOUR TOOL & GO TO IT ~ HAVE FUN! LET COMPOUND DRY FOR 24 HOURS.

APPLY PRIMER TO WALL BEFORE PAINTING SO COMPOUND DOESN'T SOAK UP THE PAINT YOU'RE ABOUT TO APPLY. PAINT WALL WITH A ROLLER DESIGNED FOR ROUGH SURFACES.

When Love adorns a home, other ornaments are secondary. ~ anonymous

HELP ME ...I'M SO TIRED....

YOU WILL NEED:

* SANDPAPER - 100 GRIT MEDIUM
* PRIMER
* PUTTY
* PAINT
* PAINT ROLLERS & BRUSHES

PREPARING THE PANELING

1. WASH WALLS SO THEY'RE FREE OF DUST & GREASE.
2. REMOVE THE FINISH ON THE PANELING BY ROUGHING UP THE SURFACE WITH SANDPAPER. LIGHTLY SAND A SMALL AREA FIRST TO MAKE SURE YOUR SANDPAPER ISN'T COARSE ENOUGH TO TEAR UP THE PANELING. USING A PALM SANDER MAKES THE SANDING JOB EASIER. WIPE DOWN WALLS TO REMOVE DUST.
3. APPLY A COAT OF PRIMER WITH A PAINT ROLLER ～ LET DRY.
4. FILL ANY NAIL HOLES WITH PUTTY. SAND FOR A SMOOTH FINISH.
5. WITH PAINT ROLLER, APPLY BASE COAT COLOR ～ LET DRY.

.... NOW ～ THE **FUN** PART !

ENHANCE YOUR NEWLY PAINTED PANELING WITH A DECORATIVE FINISH ～ UNLEASH YOUR CREATIVITY !

FINGERPAINT A FUN & FUNKY CURLY-CUE & DOT PATTERN ON YOUR KIDS' PLAYROOM WALL.

WAY COOL, MOM!

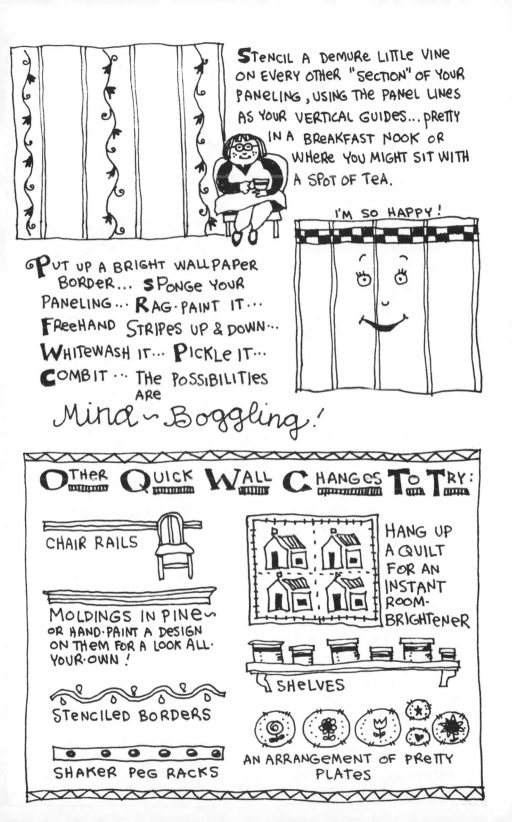

Stencil a demure little vine on every other "section" of your paneling, using the panel lines as your vertical guides... pretty in a breakfast nook or where you might sit with a spot of tea.

I'M SO HAPPY!

Put up a bright wallpaper border... **S**ponge your paneling... **R**ag·paint it... **F**reehand stripes up & down... **W**hitewash it... **P**ickle it... **C**omb it ... the possibilities are

Mind~Boggling!

Other **Q**uick **W**all **C**hanges **T**o **T**ry:

CHAIR RAILS

MOLDINGS IN PINE~ OR HAND·PAINT A DESIGN ON THEM FOR A LOOK ALL· YOUR·OWN!

STENCILED BORDERS

SHAKER PEG RACKS

HANG UP A QUILT FOR AN INSTANT ROOM· BRIGHTENER

SHELVES

AN ARRANGEMENT OF PRETTY PLATES

THE COUNTRY FRIENDS™
DECORATING
WITH
BASKETS
and
WREATHS

We love 'em! They're easily changed with the seasons and give your rooms a whole new look in a flash.

IN Fall & Winter,

CHOOSE BASKETS & WREATHS WITH A RUSTIC LOOK SUCH AS GRAPEVINE OR TWIG. DECORATE WITH:

- PINECONES
- FALL LEAVES
- BIRD FEATHERS
- BERRIES & NUTS
- EVERGREEN BOUGHS
- GILDED FRUIT

IN Spring & Summer,

SELECT LIGHTER WILLOW OR WICKER BASKETS & WREATHS. SOME ADDED TOUCHES:

- FLOWERS
- IVY GARLANDS & MOSSES
- GARDEN GLOVES & SMALL TOOLS
- SUMMER FRUITS
- LACE RIBBONS
- SEED PACKETS

Mary Elizabeth has a grapevine wreath in the kitchen decorated with cinnamon sticks & dried apple slices. Teeny little baskets are tied on the wreath with jute... cute!

Kate's sewing basket has buttons glued all around the edge, and is filled with plastic foam balls covered with long strips of plaid homespun rag.
(she can't sew a lick — what did you expect to find in her sewing basket? Thread? Needles?)

Holly displays her baskets on her wide staircase ↪ a basket on every step!

BASKET LADY

22

THE CHALLENGE: 4 SEASONS AND A FIRE-PLACE MANTEL

Oh, how Holly LOVES a decorating challenge! Watch her tackle a mantel for every season... hint: she uses items from around the house you might not normally associate with the fireplace... you try it, too!

SPRING:

- OLD LACE TABLECLOTH
- BIRDHOUSES & NESTS
- FLORAL OR GARDEN PICTURES
- GRAPEVINE GARLANDS
- VINTAGE WATERING CANS
- CLAY POTS
- TOPIARIES
- CONCRETE OR TERRACOTTA STATUES
- OLD GARDEN GATE OR WIRE FENCING
- LIGHT-COLORED BASKETS
- GARDEN TOOLS & BENCHES
- IVY
- FRAMED SEED PACKETS

SUMMER

- CROCKS
- AGED WHITE ARCHITECTURAL ITEMS
- MIRRORS
- WHITE-WASHED TWIG STARS
- CHECKED FABRIC OR TABLECLOTH
- WHITE CORDING TO LOOP ACROSS MANTEL WITH TASSELED ENDS
- OLD LANTERNS
- FLOWERS LIKE POPPIES, DAISIES, BLACK-EYED SUSANS
- FLAGS & AMERICANA

FALL:

HARVEST GARLAND
BEESWAX CANDLES
COPPER STARS
TWIGGY BRANCHES OF
    BITTERSWEET

TWIG BASKET OR
CORNUCOPIA OF PEARS,
APPLES, GOURDS, PUMPKINS

GRAPEVINE WREATH
THEOREM PAINTING
RICH VELVET OR HOMESPUN
    MANTEL CLOTH
GILDED POTS FOR WOOD
PITCHERS OR PLATES WITH
    FRUIT OR VEGGIE MOTIFS

WINTER:

CANDLES
EVERGREEN SWAGS
PINECONES
HOLIDAY COLLECTIBLES
SUCH AS SANTAS,
    SNOWMEN & ANGELS
STOCKINGS & MITTENS
MINIATURE DECORATED
    TREES
SNOWFLAKES
WREATHS
ORNAMENTS
CANDY CANES &
    PEPPERMINTS
POMANDERS
SEASONAL FLOWERS
    LIKE POINSETTIAS
    & PAPER WHITES
BOWLS OF FRUIT &
    NUTS
YULE LOG
GINGERBREAD HOUSES

A New Life for Old Lampshades

VOILÁ! QUICK CHANGES!

Smooth lampshades can be painted or sponged with a contrasting color.

Add a gathered skirt of fabric or lace to your shade.

Crocheted doilies & ribbon roses add romance!

Glue fabric appliqué designs onto lampshades.

Make a tissue paper pattern, then use spray adhesive to cover an old shade with new fabric.

Tassel trim is nice... so are gold charms. Glue 'em on!

Rubber stamp a border on your shade.

Cover a shade with a natural fiber paper embedded with flower petals.

Decoupage copies of old family photos on a tired shade for a nostalgic look.

Never under-estimate the power of a decorative sticker!

Glue on bright buttons.

Nature's mighty law is change.

-ROBERT BURNS-

New trims can be added in a flash — try lace or rickrack.

See? I can't help it. Redecorating is a force of nature.

KATE'S JAR SHELF

...a great idea for kitchen, tool bench or hobby room! Get organized!

YOU WILL NEED:

- UNFINISHED WOODEN SHELF
- CLEAN JARS WITH LIDS (JAM JARS, PICKLE JARS, OLIVE JARS, BABY FOOD JARS)
- PENCIL
- AWL
- SCREWS OR NAILS, NO LONGER THAN DEPTH OF SHELF
- HAMMER OR SCREWDRIVER

STEP 1. STAIN OR PAINT SHELF AS DESIRED. THE OUTSIDE OF THE JAR LIDS MAY ALSO BE PAINTED WITH A NON-TOXIC PAINT.

STEP 2. TO DETERMINE PLACEMENT OF THE JAR LIDS, TURN THE SHELF SO THAT THE UNDERSIDE IS FACING UP. ARRANGE LIDS SO THAT THERE IS ENOUGH ROOM TO SCREW THE JARS ON & OFF EASILY. USE A PENCIL TO MARK PLACEMENT.

STEP 3. IF YOU PLAN TO USE SCREWS, MAKE A SMALL HOLE WITH THE AWL FIRST. SECURE LIDS TO SHELF WITH SCREWS OR NAILS ∼ ABOUT 2 SHOULD DO IT.

STEP 4. ATTACH JARS TO LIDS. HANG UP SHELF, AND FILL JARS WITH NUTS, BOLTS, NAILS, BUTTONS, CANDY, BEANS... WHATEVER SMALL STUFF YOU NEED TO ORGANIZE!

One of the advantages of being DISORDERLY is that one is always making EXCITING discoveries. ∼aa milne

KATE'S
Look *
what *
I · did ·
all ·
by *
myself ·
curtain
tricks

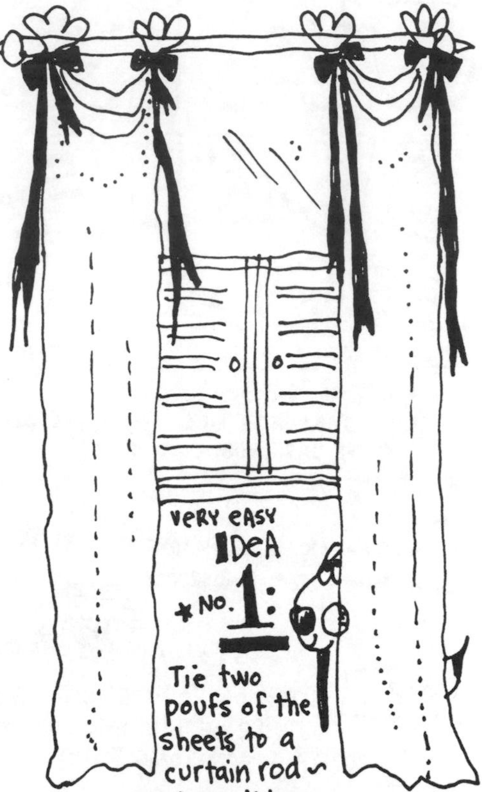

IT WAS NOTHING, really.

No sewing required!

THANK GOODNESS.

YOU DON'T HAVE TO BE A SEWING WHIZ TO MAKE WONDERFUL WINDOW TREATMENTS. (Kate is living proof of that.)

VERY EASY
IDEA
* NO. 1:

Tie two poufs of the sheets to a curtain rod ~ use long ribbon streamers! Pretty!

(Don't worry if the curtains are too long ~ just let them "puddle" up dramatically on the floor.)

HERE ARE THE BASIC INGREDIENTS:

- 2 TWIN-SIZE SHEETS
- PILLOWCASE
- RIBBON
- FUSIBLE WEB OR HEM TAPE.

(That's it!)

HOW ABOUT THIS ONE?

★ IDEA NO. 2:

Make a casing on pillowcase with fusible webbing. Insert a tension rod ~ hang it in window. Now, make a casing on the sheets using that webbing stuff again. (don't panic ~ you can do it!) OK ~ insert a rod into casing and hang the curtains. Place a small cup hook on each side of the window, about halfway down, and draw each curtain back with a pretty ribbon tie-back. Secure on the hooks.

YOU DID IT!

★ ON TO IDEA NO. 3:

SKIP THE LONG PANELS. JUST DO THE PILLOW-CASE VALANCE PART OF IDEA NO. 2!

CHECK THIS ONE OUT!

★ IDEA NO. 4:

Drape the sheet like a swag across the top of the window. Use your trusty old cup holder hooks to attach each corner!

HERE'S A NEAT
★ IDEA NO. 5:

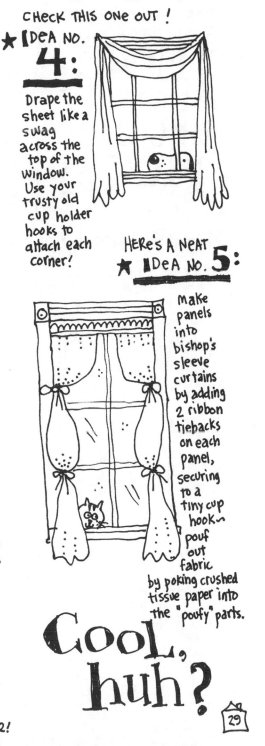

Make panels into bishop's sleeve curtains by adding 2 ribbon tiebacks on each panel, securing to a tiny cup hook ~ pouf out fabric by poking crushed tissue paper into the "poufy" parts.

Cool, huh?

There's no stopping her! She's on a roll!

MORE No*Sew Curtain Tricks!
BY * KATE *

Other Great window ideas:

IN PLACE OF CURTAINS, TRY ⤵

SHUTTERS

WOODEN GINGERBREAD TRIMS

HERB Garlands

BUNDLES OF DRIED **FLOWERS** TIED ON A LONG TREE BRANCH ↝ A NATURAL VALANCE!

GRAPEVINE Garlands

Herbs in a windowbox inside the house

SIMPLE *IDEA NO. **6:** Drape a pretty lace tablecloth over a curtain rod for a delicate look.

OK, HERE'S A GREAT THOUGHT! *IDEA NO. **7.** Tie a long piece of jute across a window. Use wooden clothespins to clip plaid kitchentowels up to the jute "curtain rod."... a perfect primitive window treatment!

I LIKE THESE **PICKET FENCE SHUTTERS.**

TIE LONG PIECES OF SATIN RIBBON TO A WOODEN DOWEL ROD FOR A SHIMMERY CURTAIN!

To be happy at home is the ultimate result of all ambition.

~ Samuel Johnson
1709 - 1784

PAINT PIZZAZZ

can't find just the right color or pattern in the correct fabric?

Print your own!

Follow Holly's tips to turn plain cotton fabric into one-of-a-kind designer fabric...

YOU WILL NEED:

- Desired amount of cotton fabric for your project (start small ~ pillows or placemats are easy and fun to use)
- textile medium
- paint brushes
- acrylic paints
- removable fabric marker

1. Wash & dry fabrics. Do not use fabric softener.

2. Mix 1 part textile medium with 2 parts acrylic paint. (Textile medium turns acrylics into paint that is washable & permanent on fabric.)

3. For plaids & intricate designs, you may want to use fabric marker & a ruler ~ otherwise, start painting!

4. Let paint dry overnight. Place a thin towel or pressing cloth on top of design ~ heat set with a hot dry iron (no steam) on cotton setting for 15 to 20 seconds. Don't scorch it now!

5. Gently wash fabric with cold water & mild soap to remove marker traces.

Green up your home with plants!

Bring a little outdoors inside with a fern or an ivy ~ a breath of fresh air.

It is the Laugh of a baby, the song of a mother, the strength of a father. Warmth of living hearts, Light from happy eyes, Kindness, Loyalty, comradeship... Where joy is shared and sorrow eased... where even the teakettle sings from happiness. That is home.

~ ERNESTINE SCHUMANN-HEINK (1861-1936) AUSTRIAN OPERA SINGER ~